MW00809558

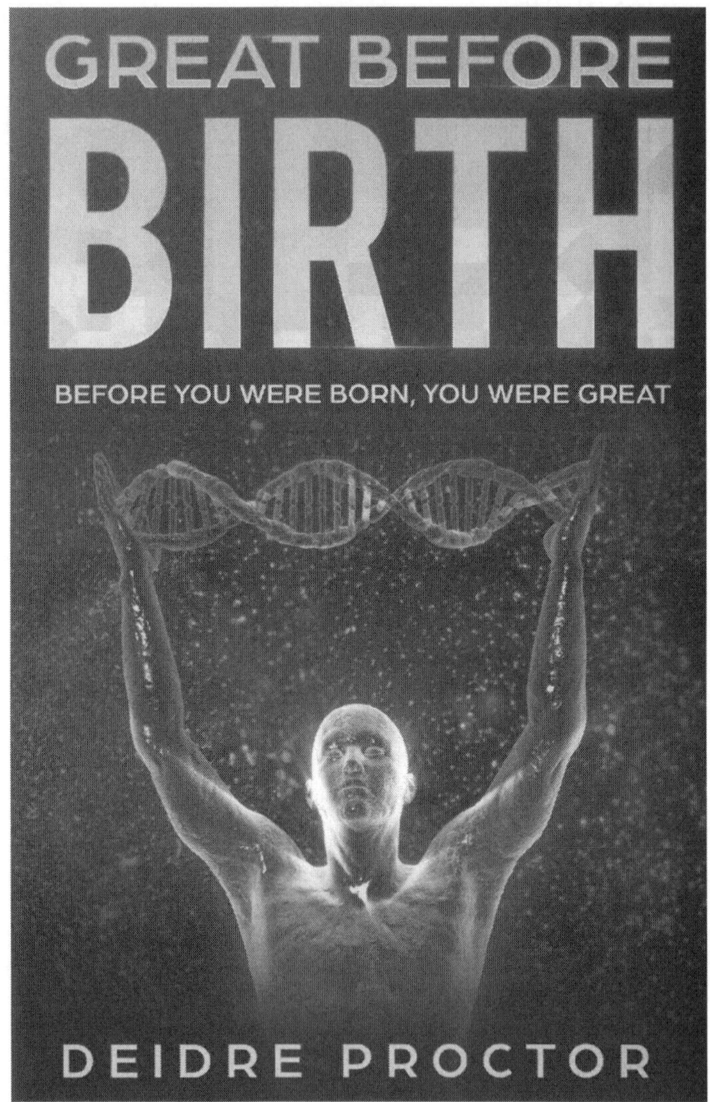
GREAT BEFORE
BIRTH
BEFORE YOU WERE BORN, YOU WERE GREAT
DEIDRE PROCTOR

GREAT BEFORE BIRTH

How To Harness The Power of God's DNA For An Extraordinary Life!

By Deidre Proctor

Great Before Birth
How To Harness The Power God's DNA For An Extraordinary Life!

This compilation is published and sold with the understanding that the author and publisher (Deidre Proctor & Associates, LLC) are not engaged in rendering legal, medical, or other professional services by reason of their authorship or publication of this work. If medical, legal, or other expert assistance is required, the services of a competent professional should be sought.

ISBN: 978-0-9832611-2-4
1st edition, July 2021
Printed in the United States of America

Dedication

- dp-

My Parents

Dedicated to the memory of my adoptive parents, Isiah and Florence Williford. Mommy you introduced me to my Heavenly Father and showed me who I really belonged to. Daddy you taught me by real life experiences what it means to lean on a father, trust and depend on a father. And, how to accept the love of a father through all the obstacles life may throw at you.

Both of you will remain in my heart forever and never be forgotten. The good thing, you are only a thought away...

Acknowledgments

-dp-

This work is a mission of the heart. I am forever grateful to my awesome husband, David, who is my best friend, supporter, champion, proofreader, intercessor, and love of my life. Thank you for giving me the inspiration to complete this book.

Thank you to our sons (John and Sterling) and daughter (Tiffany) who inspire me as I watch you grow every day in your faith.

Thank you, Pastor Bruce, and Ruth Menefee, for sharing your adoption story and pictures with me, and for always believing in and encouraging me.

And above all, I thank the source and supplier of all my wisdom, gifts, skills, talents, and love for others, God, my Father, the Creator of the Universe. I thank my Father and His Son, my elder Brother, Jesus Christ, for loving me before I was born. Thank you for allowing me to be a child of the King and servant in your Family, in your Kingdom.

Table of Contents

Foreword

by Pastor Bruce Menefee

It took me exactly a nano-second to agree to write a forward for my friend Deidre Proctor's book, Great Before Birth! I am grateful to contribute to her and her husband, David, because I have seen them contribute spiritually to many over these past 7 years that I have known them.

The Proctors have a legacy of helping people make friends and grow spiritually through small groups in our church, mentoring women's leaders, and hosting spiritual retreats for the community.

Perhaps there are a few things about this author that you need to know before you embrace this book. It may help you digest some of its rich ingredients.

First of all, Deidre is not afraid to dream! As I say that, I mean that I have watched her live what she has written in this book. She has faithfully followed a dream that she received and seen it come to fruition of ministry. The restful, and spiritually renewing retreats that she hosts are one example...and this book is still another.

Secondly, the foundations of this book will lead you to places where Deidre frequents: The Word of God and prayer. I enjoyed my journey through this book as I reviewed scriptures that have meant so much to me and my family over the years. These truths are based on solid ground of the Bible, and they are as vital to us today as the moment that they were written.

My wife Ruth, our daughter Abi, and Deidre Proctor have something very important in common. They have been twice adopted! First, physically from one family to the other, and then Spiritually into the family of God. Who we belong to sets our identity, and as this book eloquently points out, it leads to a brighter future than we can possibly imagine.

Ruth has taught me so much about the love of God through adoption and through our marriage of over 25 years. In fact, the fun didn't stop with us, but we were given the grace to adopt a daughter from Colombia after having two biologically. Do you know what we found in the process? We love all our children equally because they are all ours! How much greater is God's love than ours? He "rebirths" us into his family and adopts us into His name.

As Deidre shows us in this journey, we are sentenced to Life when we belong to our heavenly Father. Deidre's story inspires us all to see how important we are to God, and how scripture teaches that we have a purpose. In fact, she teaches that God made His decision about accepting us into Himself before we were ever born.

I want to encourage you to take a deep seat and ponder each truth through Deidre's personal story as well as the Word of God. The thought provoking questions that this work provides help us interact with Truth, and not just hear it only.

Thank you, Deidre, for such an important and insightful look at the love of God through the miracle of adoption. I love that you have found a home in Him, and love that you have helped us on that same journey.

Pastor Bruce Menefee

Introduction

~ dp ~

Before you were born, you were great. You came from royal DNA. Your lineage includes the richest and the wisest men and women the world has ever known or seen. You were born with an inheritance. You were destined to live a victorious life.

However, we find ourselves, at times, feeling the pain of despair, or brokenness, or simply frustrated with life. Financial woes, health issues, relationships in turmoil, death… all tearing down our walls of belief and confidence. We even take on our children's mistakes by blaming ourselves and convincing ourselves we were not the perfect or best father or mother we could have been.

We think about the mistakes we've made in the past, years after we made them. We find our faith diminishing. You start believing that you are alone, you're a failure, no one gets you and you're not worthy of a win. You feel like the pain will never leave. The last thing you are thinking about is your glorious heritage and your God-given legacy.

I am here today to tell you to look up and raise your head up high. Uncover your heart, remove that shield. There is so much untapped potential, purpose, and passion inside of you. You just need to seek God and ask Him for His pre-destined plan for your life.

Take Courage. If you open your heart to Him with no fear and no doubt, you will hear His voice. He is waiting on you. He is ready to bestow supernatural blessings, gifts, and talents on and through you. He truly desires that your cup of blessings has an unending flow.

I believe God is going to give you revelations as you read through this book. That is why after every chapter there are questions and a place for you to jot down your notes and thoughts.

This book is going to take you on a journey. Beginning with the beginning. And ending by you understanding your full potential and knowledge of who you really are, but more importantly, whose you really are. You will also learn how to live and walk in the fullness of the power God gifted you. I hope you are as excited as I am. Are you ready?

Let the journey begin...

Chapter 1
In The Beginning
(The Power Of The Creator)

-dp-

Before you were born, there was another beginning. In fact, before your parents, their parents, and their parents and so on and on… there was another beginning. There was the first beginning. An especially important beginning. The Bible tells us that

"In the beginning God created the heavens and the earth..." Genesis 1:1

The “Creation” phase of the Bible (Genesis 1 thru 11) is the true foundation of our existence. By the way, in those chapters you can meet some of your amazing ancestors (Adam, Eve, Enoch, Noah and so many more). All through the new and old Testaments God reveals his plan for your life using your lineage.

But let’s go back, further back than Adam and Eve. Remember, that verse begins with “In the beginning God...”. Hmmmmm…

How on earth could we be great before birth?
Where did that possibility even come from?
Who or what could possibly make that happen?

What would that person or team have to possess in order to plan it out, move obstacles, and make miracles happen in order for us to achieve the greatness that was destined just for us BEFORE we were born, even before Adam was born?

They would have to be omnibenevolent, omnipotent, omnipresent, and omniscient. Well…GOD, of course!

No team or volunteers needed. Let's take a moment and talk about the power of God, the power of the Master and Creator of the Universe. The power of our Father.

Let me share with you the magnitude of the type of power God created in the beginning so you will have a better understanding on why the life he has destined for you is so achievable and magnificent. And why He has the credentials, power, and authority to make it happen.

Think about the Universe He created---in 6 days. I can't even grow a good garden in a season. Six days people! Let me tell you what He did on just 3 of those 6 days. Check out these facts:

"16 God made two great lights—the greater light to govern the day and the lesser light to govern the night. He also made the stars.

17 God set them in the vault of the sky to give light on the earth," Genesis 1:16-17

Let me give you a glimpse of the kind of supernatural

power our Father has and take a look at those 2 “lights” He created:

- Our sun, the nearest star, is around 92 million miles away (one of the great lights).

- Compared to Earth; the Sun is enormous! It contains 99.86% of all of the mass of the entire Solar System.

- The Sun is 864,400 miles (1,391,000 kilometers) across. This is about 109 times the diameter of Earth. The Sun weighs about 333,000 times as much as Earth. It is so large that about 1,300,000 planet Earths can fit inside of it.

- The Moon is one of the most significant objects in the night sky, second only in brightness to the Sun (the other great light). The Moon is an average of 238,855 miles away from Earth, which is about 30 Earths away.

- Our universe is so vast that it would take 200,000 years for a spaceship traveling at the speed of light to go across our entire galaxy (the Milky Way).

- Our galaxy is only one among many billions in the known universe. "While estimates among different experts vary, an acceptable range is between 100 billion and 200 billion galaxies", said Mario Livio, an astrophysicist at the Space Telescope Science Institute in Baltimore.

Who do you know that has THAT kind of power? Write their name below (I'll wait).

____

____

"10 God called the dry ground "land," and the gathered waters he called "seas." And God saw that it was good.

11 Then God said, "Let the land produce vegetation: seed-bearing plants and trees on the land that bear fruit with seed in it, according to their various kinds." And it was so.

12 The land produced vegetation: plants bearing seed according to their kinds and trees bearing fruit

with seed in it according to their kinds. And God saw that it was good.

13 And there was evening, and there was morning—the third day." Genesis 1:10-13

- Earth is the fifth largest planet in the Solar System. The Diameter of the Earth is 12,756 km (7,926 miles). The earth's orbital speed is 29.8 km per second (66,660 mi/hr).

- "In 2015, a study found that there are likely more than 3 trillion individual trees on the planet, significantly more than the 400 billion previously proposed. Last summer, ecologists combed natural history specimens to find that the Amazon Basin has at least 11,676 species of trees, estimating that roughly 4,000 species in the area have yet to be discovered."

- About 71 percent of the Earth's surface is water-covered, and the oceans hold about 96.5 percent of all Earth's water. If you took all the water on Earth and put it into a ball, it would be about 860 miles wide.

Who do you know that has THAT kind of power and authority? Write their name below.

____

____

"27 So, God created mankind in his own image, in the image of God he created them; male and female he created them.

28 God blessed them and said to them, "Be fruitful and increase in number: fill the earth and subdue it. Rule over the fish in the sea and the birds in the sky and over every living creature that moves on the ground.

29 Then God said, "I give you every seed-bearing plant on the face of the whole earth and every tree that has fruit with seed in it. They will be yours for food.

30 And to all the beasts of the earth and all the birds in the sky and all the creatures that move along the ground—everything that has the breath of life in it—I give every green plant for food." And it was so.

31 God saw all that he had made, and it was very good. And there was evening, and there was morning—the sixth day. Genesis 1:27-31

- Current world population as of this second (while I am writing this paragraph) is 7,832,628,868.

- The UN estimates that around 385,000 babies are born each day around the world (140 million a year). This number will remain relatively stable in the 50 years from 2020 to 2070.

- World population is expected to reach 8 billion people in 2023 according to the United Nations.

- Today, there are millions of animal species which includes Invertebrates and Vertebrates. Although only 1.4 million species have been identified, there are somewhere between 8 and 5 million animal species estimated to be alive today.

Who do you know that has THAT kind of power, THAT kind of authority, THAT kind of originality and THAT kind of vision?

Who? GOD! I believe you understand what I am getting at. This is just a glimpse of what your Father's resume includes. Naturally, there is a TON of more facts just about the Earth, Sun and Moon. And let's not even get into the subject about the intricacies of the human body. But if he only created and birthed the details of what I just shared with you, if that is all He did, you should be in awe of the power that can be found in you.

"Ah, Sovereign Lord, you have made the heavens and the earth by your great power and outstretched arm. Nothing is too hard for you." Jeremiah 32:17

"God's power over the physical creation is absolute, such that He can manipulate matter, energy, space, and time at will. For this reason, God is said to be all powerful—able to accomplish any possible task He wills to do." Rich Deem

God's power is not limited to our physical creation. No, not all. His power is inherent within Himself. God spoke and the universe was. His power is eternal. There are no human words that can give justice to the description of His power.

Any level of power that man has; God gave it to him. There is no power that we possess that can stand against the power of God. God has the kind of power that never lets Him fail. Whatever He speaks, whatever He commands comes to pass.

There is nothing too hard for Him to accomplish. If He thinks it, it is. And here is the awesome news, this power is passed on to you, His children.

"Now to him who is able to do immeasurably more than all we ask or imagine, according to his power that is at work within us," Ephesians 3:20

Your DNA starts with our Father, God. A Father that created the Heavens and the Earth. A Father that created Mankind. A Father with the DNA that includes power, authority, command, and vision all at infinite levels. Levels that exceed our knowledge.

This is YOUR DNA! This is the blood that flows through your spiritual veins. You were not an afterthought. This IS the beginning of YOUR greatness.

What is the Holy Spirit whispering to you, right now, after reading this chapter?

Have you considered just how powerful and all-knowing God is? How do you know?

Write down your story of just one instance that you <u>KNOW</u> it was only God that blessed you in a miraculous way during that certain situation.

____

____

____

____

____

____

____

____

____

____

____

____

____

____

____

____

____

▪

Chapter 1 Notes

Chapter 2
Hello World!
(Your Birth)

-dp-

I was born in a hospital. However, as soon as I was born, I was taken from the hospital by a stranger and put in an orphanage.

There wasn't a mom and dad holding each other and looking down at me with tears of happiness in their eyes. There were no grandparents at the hospital with their chest puffed out knowing their legacy continues.

There was no special baby outfit and cute blanket to wrap me up and take me home in. Actually, there was no home for me to go to. No pretty nursery set up for me filled with stuffed animals and pretty decorations.

And certainly, there were no baby showers to announce my arrival. No gift-giving ceremonies or celebrations for this wonderful life event. If Gender Reveal parties were a thing back then, guess who would not have gotten one? Me.

No family members surrounding my mother with love and hugs. No one laboring over choosing a name for the baby. In fact, quite the opposite.

My biological mother didn't even bother to give me a name. So, the Orphanage gave me one. They gave me my mother's name.

I had no real identity. I had no relatives to see about me. No Aunt or Grandmother to take me in. I had no one. There was nothing special about me, just another single mom statistic. I was totally dependent on the workers at the orphanage to feed me, dress me, and tend to my needs. Then put me in a crib next to the many cribs in one room.

"Though my father and mother forsake me, the Lord will receive me..." Psalm 27:10

How depressing and sad is all of that? Who gives up their baby? Who lets total strangers take their baby without a fight? Sounds bad, right?

Here is one thing I know for sure; God does not make mistakes. That is the first thing YOU have to know... no... believe. Without a shadow of a doubt, believe this, God - does - not - make – mistakes.

No matter where you found yourself at birth or who you found yourself with at birth, God does not make mistakes. People do.

And when people make those "mistakes" God steps in and turns what satan meant for evil or bad into blessings.

"You intended to harm me, but God intended it for good to accomplish what is now being done, the saving of many lives." Genesis 50:20

I believe every reader of this book can remember times in your life where what seemed to be a bad thing or bad situation in your life, ended up being the best thing that could have happened to you. You knew you were burning while you were going through the fire, but after the fire was quenched, you realized that you would not have had it any other way.

I saw a video rescue of a newborn found on the side of a country road in Forsyth, Georgia. She was tossed aside and found in a plastic bag, alive! Praise God! So even though my newborn beginning is a sad story, her story is worse, in my opinion. And there are so many other stories out there that border horrible and inhumane.

Listen, terrible things will happen to all of us. Why? Because God allows all of us to have freewill in the choices we make and because of that we live in a sinful world.

But God is always there, right by our sides, reaching out to us and waiting for us to ask for His help in dealing with whatever we are going through. He supplies us with every tool we need to conquer the issues and situations that we encounter on our journey.

Don't let people discourage you by commenting on or giving their opinion on your current or past situations. Don't believe in what they believe about you or your past, even your future. God's plan for you, that was activated at birth, is still in play. Your birth was the beginning of one of the greatest plans ever made!

God has pre-destined every person's life BEFORE they were born. It doesn't matter if you were born into a loving family, rich family, poor family, single-parent family or even if you came into this world and was dropped into a broken, hard, or horrible situation, God has already crafted the perfect plan for your life. He already knew the paths that were going to be offered to you.

He set you up to be prepared to make the hard choices, the fast choices and even the simple choices, but the right choices, when the time came.

"My Father's house has many rooms; if that were not so, would I have told you that I am going there to prepare a place for you?" John 14:2

Now we know that everything that happens is not God's will. If you go over the speed limit, then get pulled over by a policeman and given a ticket, was that God's fault? No, of course not. But once you made your choice to speed, God's plan for you was redirected. Just like a GPS... He re-routes us.

He is still directing us towards Heaven, to live with him, to claim our mansion, but our choices determine our path and how we get there.

However, there are some circumstances and events that God does allow because it is in His plan. Though we don't always understand His plans, we must always trust His plans.

My son and my daughter-n-love expected their first child (my first grandbaby) a few years ago. I screamed, jumped up and down and was overjoyed with happiness and excitement when they told us. The other grandmommy and siblings were all just as excited. But none more excited than the parents-to-be.

Mommy was in good health and Daddy was taking care of her well. I knew they would be great parents. However, not long into the pregnancy, there was a miscarriage. All of our hearts were saddened.

But we knew that we would see our grandchild again, because we had faith like David (2 Samuel 12: 23). A year later my son and daughter-n-love were blessed with a beautiful baby girl! Plan activated!

See my precious grandbaby on the next page.

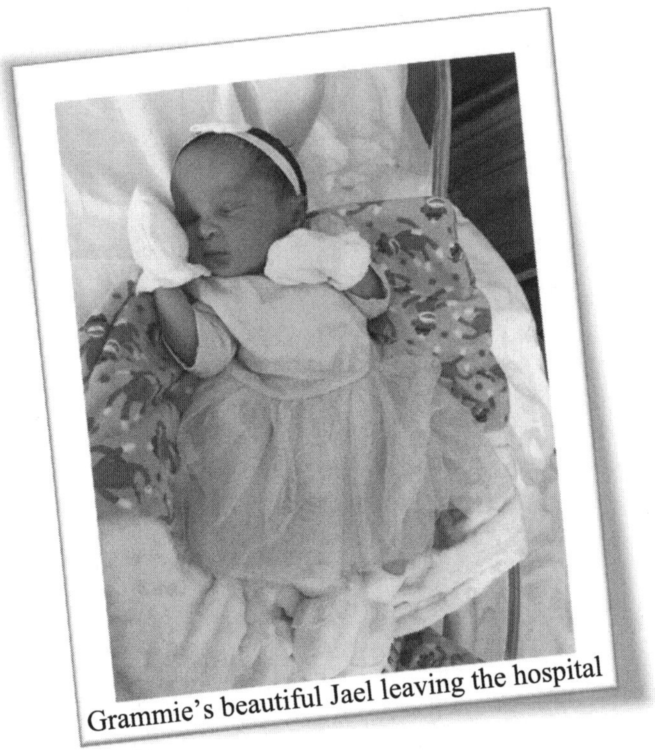
Grammie's beautiful Jael leaving the hospital

I do not believe it was God's will for my mother to "hook up" with a guy and get pregnant, but since she chose to do that, He used her choice to deliver me into this world and set my path on becoming who I am today.

She could have chosen to abort me (another choice) but I am thankful to my birth mother for choosing to give me life. That was the first best decision “man” ever made for my life.

The moment that your mother and father conceived you, the moment that egg and sperm connected, your pre-destined plan was activated. Your life’s journey kicked into action. At this point, you have no control of your life. There is no interference from you. No choices for you to make. The choices your parents/guardians make will align with God’s will or not.

But His plan is yet in play. His direction for your life, regardless of their choices, are yet set before you. I had no choice in who birthed me nor into what circumstances I was delivered into. But God was still utterly and completely in control of my life.

So now, you made it into your new world, you have arrived, the baby has come forth, what now?

What is the Holy Spirit whispering to you, right now, after reading this chapter?

Remind yourself of a time in your life when you found yourself in a terrible predicament, but that situation ended up being the best thing that could have happen to you.

Chapter 2 Notes

Chapter 3
Oh No! You Were Adopted!
(Your Adoption)

-dp-

My adoptive Mom had a hysterectomy early in her life and therefore could not bear children. She and my dad had been married for several years before they decided to adopt a child.

The day they made the decision to adopt, they also made the decision that they wanted a son. My mother wanted my dad to have a son, one she could not give him. (At that time, my Dad did not know that he had fathered a son 18 years earlier. We will talk about my wonderful brother a little later).

When my parents walked into my orphanage, they told the Director that they would like to adopt a baby boy. As my mother was speaking to the woman in charge, the woman looked over my mother's shoulder and said, "I think you might be going home with a baby girl instead of a baby boy".

My mother immediately turned around saw my dad on the floor, smiling big and playing with a baby girl! The baby girl was laughing and cooing right back.

Immediately, on the spot, they made a choice to change their mind about adopting a baby boy, they were going to bring home that baby girl, me! Little did they know that God's plan for my life had already been in play, and they were a part of that plan.

That one decision, that one choice, changed their lives and my life forever. It was the 2nd best decision made for my life. Praise the Lord, God was still in control.

Let me interject this right now: no matter who your parents are/were, no matter if you never had parents and were raised in the sometime terrible but necessary Foster System, the choices you make as an adult are all yours.

So, you were adopted, or raised by your grandparents or other relatives, or raised by strangers. Take note that we are all adopted! Let's talk about that.

ADOPTION IS PART OF GOD'S MASTER PLAN.

Did you know Moses was adopted (Exodus 2:1-10)? Esther was adopted by her cousin after her parents' deaths. Even Jesus was adopted! Joseph adopted Jesus and raised him as his own son with Mary. God wants us all to become a part of His family. This is our spiritual family.

"He predestined us for adoption to sonship through Jesus Christ, in accordance with his pleasure and will-" Ephesians 1:5

Your inheritance is readily accessible to you once you ask to be officially adopted into His family.

"Because you are his sons, God sent the Spirit of his Son into our hearts, the Spirit who calls out, "Abba, Father..." Galatians 4:6

You don't have to wait until you get a certain age before it is available to you. God knew you before your birth, in fact, the Bible tells us that he formed us and released us with a purpose and a plan.

"The word of the Lord came to me, saying, "Before I formed you in the womb, I knew you, before you were born, I set you apart;
Jeremiah 1:4-5

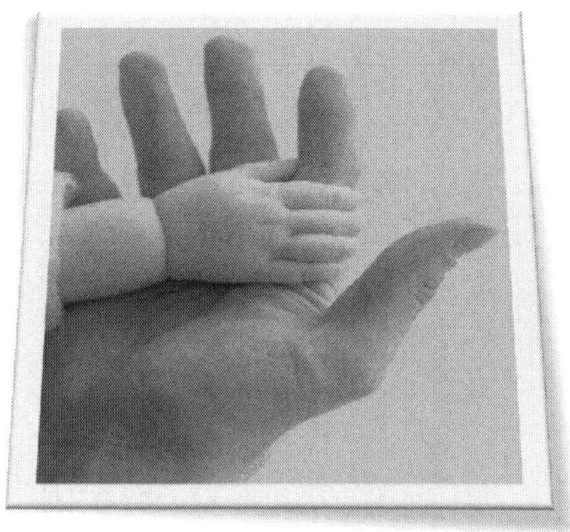

Let's look at some of the differences between Spiritual Adoption and Natural Adoption:

NATURAL ADOPTION	SPIRITUAL ADOPTION
• Benefits/resources are limited.	• Benefits/resources are Eternal.
• Is usually limited in the size of the adoptive family due to finances or the limited number of children the parents want.	• Brings you into a heavenly family of brothers and sisters all over the world and even the Angels in Heaven.
• No guaranteed legacy from parents.	• Guaranteed legacy from God.
• You do not get the DNA of the adoptive parents.	• You instantly get the DNA of God, our Father.

Naturally, there are more differences, but I believe those are the top 4. The best point, however, is that when God adopts you... you get His DNA!

The point is this: you may come from a two-parent, rich, highly educated family, but if you have not accepted your true inheritance from God, you are living waaaayyyy below your means. You are living and walking in a poor life.

You are doing a disservice to your family and everyone in your life by not realizing or accepting your place in God's family. You are doing a disservice to all those that God could use you to reach with his bountiful blessings.

You are doing a disservice to yourself!

When God
Adopts You,
You Get His
DNA! dp

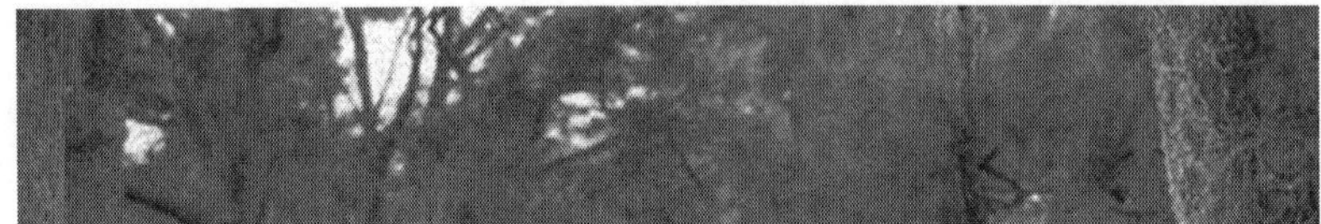

Wait...STOP!

If you have not accepted Jesus Christ as your Lord and Savior, I want to take this moment to invite you into the family. Don't worry about if you will fit in this family. Or think that you are not good enough to be a part of this royal family.

God wanted you in His family before you were born. He knew you would be born into a sinful world. So, he already knew that you would have to want to make a choice to be in His family or stay in the ruler of the sinful world's family. The choice is yours.

KNOW THESE TRUTHS AND MAKE THESE SIMPLE STEPS:

Jesus Christ is the only Way to salvation. That way is through faith in Him.

- Agree with God that all have sinned, which includes you and me. Yes, every person in His family has sinned, except for His 1st born, Christ.

"for all have sinned and fall short of the glory of God," Romans 3:23

- Know that the gift of salvation, the price to be adopted into God's family, is free.

"For the wages of sin is death, but the gift of God is eternal life in Christ Jesus our Lord." Romans 6:23

- Ask for forgiveness. Ask God to forgive you for all of your sins. Then BELIEVE that He will and has.

"If we confess our sins, he is faithful and just and will forgive us our sins and purify us from all unrighteousness." 1 John 1:9

"For, Everyone who calls on the name of the Lord will be saved." Romans 10:13

And now the GOOD NEWS for all of us:

"But now that you have been set free from sin and have become slaves of God, the benefit you reap leads to holiness, and the result is eternal life." Romans 6:22

Welcome to the Family!

What is the Holy Spirit whispering to you, right now, after reading this chapter?

Have you accepted Jesus as your Lord and Savior?

____

____

Do you currently serve or would eventually like to serve in the family (prayer intercessor, hospitality, working with children, single-parents, youth, young adults, seniors, home bible study groups, outreach, missions, etc.)?

____

____

____

Why did you choose that need to fill?

____

____

____

____

____

____

____

____

____

____

____

____

Chapter 3 Notes

Chapter 4
A Loving Family
(Your Family)

-dp-

As long as I can remember, I have known I was adopted. My parents told me I was adopted when I was a little girl. However, I never had those moments as a child or teen to wonder who and where were my biological parents because my adoptive parents gave me so much love. They took care of my physical needs, my wants, and disciplined me when necessary. They poured into me what they knew of the love of God. They taught me the meaning of family.

When God placed me in my new family, that initiated the next phase of His plan for my life. I call this stage my growth and learning stage.

Every good thing that happened in the first 21 years of my life and every mistake and every bad choice I made during that time, taught me life lessons (that is another book for another time). But while I was experiencing all of life's ups and downs, my good and bad choices, through tears and laughter, my family (even my extended family) was right by my side. They celebrated with me and held no judgement against me. Their love for me was unconditional.

When you are adopted in God's Family, your life is changed forever. It will never be the same. You will never be alone again. Your support system is now through the roof! That support system includes your church home, your prayer partners, your sisters and brothers in Christ and, of course, the Trinity (God, Jesus and The Holy Spirit). You are forever loved unconditionally.

Unconditional love. What does that mean for you? It means that there is nothing, NOTHING, that you can do or nothing that is done to you that will make God stop loving you.

35 Who shall separate us from the love of Christ? Shall trouble or hardship or persecution or famine or nakedness or danger or sword?

38 For I am convinced that neither death nor life, neither angels nor demons, neither the present nor the future, nor any powers,

39 neither height nor depth, nor anything else in all creation, will be able to separate us from the love of God that is in Christ Jesus our Lord. Romans 8:35, 38-39

When you let God adopt you, you then are brought into a huge family. God's family. I was not brought into a large adoptive family unit. It was just me, my Dad, and Mom. It was wonderful. However, when I was 8 years old, my Dad found out he had an 18 year old son, Curley. My Dad asked him to come stay with us after he graduated from High School.

Dad got Curley a summer job working at the Steel Mill with him. I was beyond thrilled that I, an only child, had a big brother coming to live with us.

I could not wait for him to arrive. I would have someone to play with, brag about to my friends, be my best friend, my protector, and all the other ideas a little girl has about a big brother. (Ok, so playing with me and my dolls didn't quite work out like I pictured in my mind).

My brother, Curley

When my Mom and I went to the train station to pick him up, I noticed him first, because he looked just like my Dad and was way over 6 feet tall! I fell in love at first sight.

I remember the days, while I would be outside playing, I would call him to come to our front door just so I could show him off to my elementary school friends who didn't believe I had a big brother. He would look at me with a "really Deidre" look. I loved my brother with all my heart (he passed away several years ago due to cancer).

He was my only brother and I still miss him tremendously. But I had to realize that I didn't lose my only brother.

Although I lost my earthly brother, I still had my elder, bigger, spiritual brother, Jesus. Yes, YOUR power family's eldest son is Jesus Christ, now YOUR big brother, too!

"Now if we are children, then we are heirs—heirs of God and co-heirs with Christ, if indeed

we share in his sufferings in order that we may also share in his glory." Romans 8:17

Jesus even recognizes you as his brother or sister. And He is not that jealous or competitive brother. He wants to share everything our Father gave Him with all of us.

"11 Both the one who makes people holy and those who are made holy are of the same family. So, Jesus is not ashamed to call them brothers and sisters.

12 He says, "I will declare your name to my brothers and sisters; in the assembly I will sing your praises.

13 And again, "I will put my trust in him." And again, he says, "Here am I, and the children God has given me." Hebrews 2: 11-13

We're a family in Christ. And like any family, God's family is filled with people in all stages of spiritual development: newborn believers, those still adolescent in their walk, and the spiritually mature. You are not alone.

Know this, when you are adopted in God's family, it does not mean bad or unfortunate events won't happen to you or to those you love. It does not mean you will make all the right choices, say all the right words, go to all the right places or even keep company with all the right people.

It does mean that every trial can lead to a testimony. It does mean every obstacle is just a steppingstone to your blessings. It does mean every lesson will grow you into a mature Christian. Your faith and perseverance level will increase.

Listen, the good and the bad, the saved and the unsaved, will have heart-breaking situations happen in their lives. The difference is this, God's sons and daughters who have accepted Him as their father actually have Him to turn to in rough times. Those who have not accepted Him, will go through those times without Him, alone.

If you are going to have to go through problems, anyway, wouldn't it be much better to have God on your side? The one who can fix the problem or give you the peace and courage to go through the situation.

"Let perseverance finish its work so that you may be mature and complete, not lacking anything." James 1:4

My husband and I try to have a special dinner one Sunday a month for our adult children who still live in the area. We gather together, eat, talk and laugh around the table. That is always one of the highlights of my month.

Seeing our kids laugh about old things and share what's new in their life, asking our opinions on relationships, investments, or whatever is going on in their life at the time, puts a smile on our hearts.

It is that type of wonderful and uplifting feeling you feel when you are around your spiritual family. Joining God's family is such a powerful move that the

Angels rejoice when only one brother or sister is added in the family!

WHAT CAN YOU DO TO EARN A PLACE IN GOD'S FAMILY?

According to His Word:

"5 He saved us, not because of righteous things we had done, but because of his mercy. He saved us through the washing of rebirth and renewal by the Holy Spirit,

6 Whom he poured out on us generously through Jesus Christ our Savior,

7 so that, having been justified by his grace, we might become heirs having the hope of eternal life." Titus 3:5-7

That is good news! There are no works that we can do to earn a place in the Kingdom family. We, by birth right, become living heirs to Jesus' inheritance. God's spiritual blessings are automatic and infinite. We receive this because of God's grace. But it does not stop there.

By accepting God's invitation into the family, He also gives us the indwelling of the Holy Spirit.

"13 And you also were included in Christ when you heard the message of truth, the gospel of your salvation. When you believed, you were marked in him with a seal, the promised Holy Spirit,

14 who is a deposit guaranteeing our inheritance until the redemption of those who are God's possession—to the praise of his glory. Ephesians 1:13-14

What is the Holy Spirit whispering to you, right now, after reading this chapter?

Describe a favorite childhood memory?

Why do you think that is the memory you chose?

Chapter 4 Notes

Chapter 5
Who's Your Daddy?
(Your Personal Relationship)

-dp-

We have talked about the power and authority of God. We know we have His DNA running thru our spiritual veins. We know we are adopted into His family. But do you really know your Father? Or do you still know Him as a child knows Him? Meaning, the "Yes, Jesus loves me" or "Now I lay me down to sleep..." version of Him.

Have you developed an intimate relationship with God yet? Do you talk to Him on a daily basis? Do you depend on God in the good and bad times? Do you read your bible daily?

When I was in my late 20's, I moved to Texas. I didn't call my Mom every day after the move. So, every time I did call, she would say something like, "oh, so you finally made time to call your mother", sarcastically. It didn't matter that I could have spoken to her the previous week. For her, every day was not too often.

One day, one of our sons, said this to me after I gave him some constructive criticism (or as I like to think, some motherly love), "Mom, I am a grown man." He did not say it in a disrespectful way, he just wanted to be sure I knew he could handle the situation.

There is a connection that a parent has with the children they raise. A good parent, because of that connection bond, wants to constantly hear from you, be in your life, pray for you, want nothing but good things to happen to and for you, protect you (even as an adult), and help you anyway they can. They want you to ask them for advice, listen to them, and appreciate them.

Remember, we are made in the image of God, therefore, that connection bond is just part of God's

DNA. He wants the exact same relationship with us. He wants to give us blessings that our cup cannot hold.

"If you, then, though you are evil, know how to give good gifts to your children, how much more will your Father in heaven give good gifts to those who ask him"! Matthew 7:11

God wants to have daily fellowship with His children. He wants us to cast our cares on Him, tell Him about our day, praise Him for our life and His many blessings, cry to Him in our sorrows, and lean on Him when we feel like falling down.

But who exactly is God? We acknowledge that He is the Almighty, All-knowing, Alpha and Omega, Supreme Being, Ruler, Lord, Jehovah, Our Creator.

"Then I heard what sounded like a great multitude, like the roar of rushing waters and like loud peals of thunder, shouting: "Hallelujah! For our Lord God Almighty reigns"." Revelation 19:6

But simply put, God is love. And because of His

powerful love, He created us. Created us to share and spread His love to the world.

"16 And so, we know and rely on the love God has for us. God is love. Whoever lives in love lives in God, and God in them.

17 This is how love is made complete among us so that we will have confidence on the day of judgment: In this world we are like Jesus." 1 John 4:16-17

Of course, you have heard how much he sacrificed because of His love for us. Yes, He allowed His only son to be crucified on the cross so that you and I could spend eternal life with Him. This is how badly He wants you in His family.

"For God so loved the world that he gave his one and only Son, that whoever believes in him shall not perish but have eternal life." John 3:16

And here's the thing, Jesus did not wait until we got our act together before He said yes to His Father's desire. The people were chanting for His death! Yet,

His death gave them life. This is how much our Father and Brother loves us.

Do you see and understand the depth of God's love for you, His child?

My Dad loved his only son, my brother. One day my father went to the store and bought some yellow paint to freshen up one of the rooms in our house. After the purchase, he placed the paint in the trunk of his car and drove home. He wasn't going to paint for a couple of days, so he left the paint in the trunk.

My brother asked our Dad if he could use the car. My Dad said "yes" and gave him the keys. Unfortunately, Curley had an accident while he was out. He was not hurt, thank God, but my father now had a yellow trunk.

Did Dad disown his son? No. His love for him did not waiver. I had a really good belly laugh, though.

My father taught me how to drive by letting me drive around in parking lots. Then after some time, he would let me drive from the store to home.

One day, as I was getting ready to turn into our driveway, Dad felt I was going too fast and started, quite boisterous I might say, telling me to press on the brake. Well, he made me nervous and instead of pressing on the brake, I pressed harder on the accelerator. There was a tree that sat on the corner of the driveway. You guessed it! We went straight up that tree.

My Dad got out the car and went and sat in the backyard, his back to the house. I kept peeking out the kitchen window at him. My mother told me stop worrying, he will be alright. Next week, in another car, he let me get behind the wheel again.

No matter what we did, our parents' love for us never wavered. Were we disciplined when we broke the rules? Of course! But we knew our parents loved us to the moon and back. Why? We were their children.

Remember the 'Love Is" quotes? Well, Let me tell you what and who God is by giving you a dish of "God Is" ...

God Is...

God is:

- Love
- Merciful
- Good
- Gracious
- Long-suffering
- Forgiving
- Full of Grace
- Light
- Truth
- Perfect
- Life
- Omnipotent
- Omniscient
- Omnipresent
- Righteous
- Creator
- Glorious
- Wise
- Sovereign
- Invisible (He is a Spirit)
- Immutable
- Faithful
- Just
- Infinite
- Self-Sufficient
- Gentle
- Protector
- Provider
- Kind
- Patient
- Honest
- Compassionate
- Awesome
- Amazing
- Unique
- Ever-lasting
- Holy

We don't know everything there is to know about God or even understand all there is to know about Him. We do know that God is ever present with us. We know that He is the best Father in this world and in this Universe. And we know that His DNA is our DNA.

"33 Oh, the depth of the riches of the wisdom and knowledge of God! How unsearchable his judgments, and his paths beyond tracing out!

34 "Who has known the mind of the Lord? Or who has been his counselor?"

35 "Who has ever given to God, that God should repay them?"

36 For from him and through him and for him are all things. To him be the glory forever! Amen.
Romans 11:33-36

What is the Holy Spirit whispering to you, right now, after reading this chapter?

Write your personal "God is..." truths.

God is:

____

____

____

____

____

____

____

Chapter 5 Notes

Read The Bible,
Know God's Love

Chapter 6
You Were Made For This
(Your Purpose & Passion)

-dp-

God has a deep and meaningful plan for your life. A plan that will touch many, many lives. A plan that you were created for. Every second of every moment since your birth He has been preparing you to see that plan unfold.

You are equipped, stocked, loaded and able to execute that plan. You have been created by God to serve Him and build up the Kingdom of your Father by growing His family.

Your purpose and your passion will synchronize with that plan. When you come into full realization of the plan God gifted you with, all doubt, confusion and frustration will cease. You will feel like an ignition has been started in your life. Obstacles are no longer devastating issues, just problems to be solved.

It won't matter how many no's you hear, how many negative comments are released in your presence, or how many family and friends (with good intentions) tell you that the path you are on will be too hard for you to travel.

But here's the thing: the difference between HEARING that God has a plan for you and KNOWING that He has a plan for you, that is the issue.

How do you KNOW if God even has a plan for you?

How do you KNOW that you have what it takes to execute His plan for you?

How do you KNOW if you have what it takes to see the plan through?

How do you KNOW if you are following your plan or God's plan?

How do you KNOW if you are in the will of God?

How do you KNOW if it is God's voice you are hearing?

How do you KNOW....

Write your own self-doubt(s) about following God's plan for your life and why you have those doubts:

1.

2.

3.

My first go to scripture for this chapter is:

"For I know the plans I have for you," declares the Lord, "plans to prosper you and not to harm you, plans to give you hope and a future." Jeremiah 29:11

God said it and that settles it. He has a plan for you, period. He has a plan for me, you, and all of His children. For me, that is the "drop the mic" verse. Or the "If you didn't know, now you know" verse. GOD HAS A PLAN FOR YOUR LIFE.

Once we accept the fact that God has specific plans for our lives, our hearts become open and conditioned by faith to willingly hear and listen to God's voice when the Holy spirit encourages us to take a certain action.

For example, when we feel led to buy food for the homeless, or stop what we are doing to pray for someone, or say yes to leading a Bible Study home group, or show love to the hurting, or share the good news of Jesus Christ, etc. When we are obedient, we become more and more in tune with the Holy Spirit as He guides us on a daily basis to do God's will.

How do you know His will for your life? By simply asking Him. Go to God in prayer and ask Him all the questions on your heart about His plan for your life.

"14 This is the confidence we have in approaching God: that if we ask anything according to his will, he hears us.

15 And if we know that he hears us—whatever we ask—we know that we have what we asked of him." 1 John 5:14-15

Know that when you pray to God, you are saying that you believe in Him and you are putting your trust in Him. He will answer your prayers. It may not be in the moment you ask, but He will answer your prayers. He longs to talk with you, every day. The more you make time for Him the easier it will be to hear and know His voice.

God may not reveal His plan for you right away or He may give you an understanding of your past journey and not reveal the future plan He has in store for you. Or he may even give you a glimpse of your future or send confirmations your way. But guess what? It does not matter.

What matters is that you know you have a plan and that everything you do that is in His will are steps in fulfilling that plan.

What really matters is that you seek God first, listen to what He wants to share with you and talk with Him. Have a conversation with Him. We call that, prayer time. Our special time with our Father.

"But seek first his kingdom and his righteousness, and all these things will be given to you as well." Matthew 6:33

Not only does that verse mean physical, financial, and spiritual blessings will be given to you, but it includes wisdom and knowledge which means He will guide you through the plan He has destined for your life.

Several years ago, I was the Executive Director of an online retail company. When the President of that company made changes to the company's policy, He gave the management team the plan that he wanted us to implement so the contract workers would react positively to the transitions. Sometimes those plans had been in the making for months before implementation. Sometimes, he gave us sections of the plans instead of the whole plan to implement.

However, he knew the plans were good ones and that we would implement them exactly like he had instructed us to, even though we might have not known exactly how the outcome of implementing the plan would go. He believed in our talents and skills. He knew that we had the proper training. And we trusted that he knew the plans would benefit all of us in the end. The goal was for the company to grow, and it did. And because we did our part in the Boss's plan, our rewards (bonuses) were awesome!

God knows your skills and what you are passionate about. He knows that His plans for you will align with your heart and your skills. You were created not only to worship him and spread the good news, but also to accomplish your specific given plan. Listen to His voice. You will know you are privy to His voice because the bible says,

"My sheep listen to my voice; I know them, and they follow me." John 10:27

"Whoever belongs to God hears what God says. The reason you do not hear is that you do not belong to God." John 8:47

But you may say "I am still unsure if it's God's voice speaking to me. I know He speaks to others, but how do I really know He is speaking to me?" Let me tell you how.

Just compare what you are hearing to God's Word, the scriptures. Do the two line up? Does the action "the voice" is telling you to do, or direction to follow, align with the Word of God? Remember, God will never say anything contrary to His Word.

This becomes much easier when you let scripture reading become a part of your daily routine. Psalm 119:11 states, " I have hidden your word in my heart that I might not sin against you."

I believe the more you commit God's word to your heart, the clearer and louder His voice becomes in your life. That is one reason this book is filled with scriptures.

When we use God's scriptures in our prayers, we are talking His language.

So how do you remember all of those scriptures? One scripture at a time. Remember the joke, "How do you eat an elephant? One bite at a time". Well, it is true. Don't try to memorize a chapter all at once. I suggest starting with the promises of God. The Bible Promise Book is a great resource to use to start your memorization journey.

Here are 6 additional ways to help you memorize scripture:

- ✓ Tape a different scripture each week on your refrigerator and say it out loud each morning.

- ✓ Record yourself reading scriptures, then listen to it in the car, waiting rooms, working out, etc.

- ✓ Take screen shots of your favorite online verses and create a Verse Album in your photo application on your cell.

- ✓ Listen to scriptures using an audio Bible.

- ✓ Use scripture pictures or graphics as the wallpaper on your phone or laptop.

- ✓ Write a scripture down 3 times and say it out loud 3 times.

What are some other ways you can think of to help you memorize scriptures?

____

____

____

____

____

"For the word of God is alive and active. Sharper than any double-edged sword, it penetrates even to dividing soul and spirit, joints and marrow; it judges the thoughts and attitudes of the heart." Hebrews 4:12

Will everything and everyday be peaches and cream? No, of course not! There will be doubts, difficulties, hurdles, and definitely negative voices in our head as we develop and grow in the fullness of God's desire and plan for our lives. God knew this. That is why He teaches us how to maneuver on this earth.

"14 Stand firm then, with the belt of truth buckled around your waist, with the breastplate of righteousness in place,

15 and with your feet fitted with the readiness that comes from the gospel of peace.

16 In addition to all this, take up the shield of faith, with which you can extinguish all the flaming arrows of the evil one.

17 Take the helmet of salvation and the sword of the Spirit, which is the word of God."
Ephesians 6:14-17

Why would you need the full armor of God? Because you will face adversity. You will need all of the power and authority of your Father (remember whose DNA runs in your spiritual veins) to stand against satan and all of his demonic spirits. He has provided you with all the resources you need to stand against life's natural and spiritual struggles.

Wearing the armor of God gives you the protection you will need when an attack happens. In fact, by having on the full armor of God at all times also means you will not be ambushed or be taken by surprise when you are attacked.

Our adversary is on his job. He stays on his job. He is laser-focused on his job. He attacks us every chance he gets, thru death, sickness, infidelity, losses, jealousy, broken promises, wolves in sheep clothing, and so more.

However, by wearing the armor of God means we are on our job, too! By hiding God's Word in our heart, we are on our job. By believing, having faith, and loving our Father, we are on our job. No matter how good satan is at his job, he does not come close to the power of the Almighty, our Father. And because God's DNA is our DNA, we are powerful, too. We just have to tap into our source!

WE ARE THE VICTORIOUS ONES!! OUR FAMILY WINS!!

Do you believe in yourself and ready to own the fact that God's DNA is running through your spiritual veins and that God has a plan for you?

Circle one: YES NO

Yes? Then pray this prayer:

"Father,
I know that you are the God of my life. Please forgive my sins. I believe that Jesus died on the cross for my sins. Help me to fully believe in not some, but all of your promises. Help me to believe in myself, that you truly find me worthy to be called your child. Help me to believe that you have a plan for my life. Help me to understand what you would have me do. Increase my faith, wisdom, and knowledge so I will fulfill that
plan. I give you all the thanks and praise for what you have done and are doing in my life, and I look to you for my future. I love you God and ask all of this in the name of your son, my brother, Jesus Christ.
Amen"

***If you circled NO, please go back to chapter 1 and start reading JUST the scriptures from chapter 1 thru chapter 6.

Prayer Closet
Where do you spend your
quiet time with God?

What is the Holy Spirit whispering to you, right now, after reading this chapter?

Chapter 6 Notes

Your Passion
Your Purpose

Chapter 7
Own It
(Operating In Your Greatness)

-dp-

Satan is an adversary but no longer a champion or victor in your life. He can no longer halt the plans your Father has ordained for you. It doesn't mean he is going to stop attacking you and sending obstacles, losses, and distractions your way.

However, now that you know the Greatness inside of you, now that you know whose DNA is directing and protecting you, make no mistake, the enemy will lose, fail, and eventually be thrown in the pit of hell. You Win, We WIN!

"And the devil, who deceived them, was thrown into the lake of burning sulfur, where the beast and the false prophet had been thrown. They will be tormented day and night for ever and ever." Revelation 20:10

Your every action now comes from a different perspective. There has been a shift in your life. Your eyes and heart have been opened to receive the glorious life God has specifically planned for you. You walk differently, you talk differently, you think differently, you love differently.

When you speak, you now know the power of your words and you know where that power exudes from.

"Consequently, you are no longer foreigners and strangers, but fellow citizens with God's people and also members of his household, built on the foundation of the apostles and prophets, with Christ Jesus himself as the chief cornerstone." Ephesians 2:19-20

This is your day. This is your time. This is the chapter of your life that you walk in your greatness. No holding back.

The fight to live thru and above any circumstances is now in your ballpark. You can choose to sit back, wallow and whine because of your life or you can stand up and fight like the warrior inside of you wants to do.

This is the time to show the world what you are made of. Time to tell the world who you are and whose you are. Because now your steps are directed by God.

"***The Lord makes firm the steps of the one who delights in him;***

24 though he may stumble, he will not fall,
for the Lord upholds him with his hand."
Psalm 37: 23-24

Will you get weary at times? Yes! I host a sold-out Christian women's retreat every year in Texas called The Breathe Retreat. The ladies come to be refreshed and rejuvenated. Why? Because we all get weary and tired at some point. But you have the power to renew, rejuvenate and refocus.

Let's face it, you are probably weary because you have relied on your own abilities instead of your Father's power. We are to rely on His power within us.

I remember there was a big winter storm in North Texas this year (believe it or not) and there was a huge power outage. All the king's horses and all the king's men couldn't turn that power back on immediately.

In some areas, even the water became contaminated because the pumps filters stopped working and we were warned not to use or drink the water for a couple of days. All because of the power outage.

Friends, I have good news for you, God never has a power outage. That power, the same power He gave Jesus, is now ours.

"But you will receive power when the Holy Spirit comes on you; and you will be my witnesses in Jerusalem, and in all Judea and Samaria, and to the ends of the earth." Acts 1:8

"Finally, be strong in the Lord and in his mighty power." Ephesians 6:10

So, now that you have accepted your place in God's family, what's next? Let me give you some starter suggestions:

CLOSENESS

When I graduated from high school, I pretty much felt I knew everything I needed to know about life and what I needed to succeed. Lord, how many of us have said "if I could start all over again" or "if I knew then what I know now...".

I do not believe I thought from one month to the next or even one week to the next. I did not utilize all of the wisdom of my parents. They were good enough to raise me, but now that I am "grown" at 16, they just were not with the times. Ha! Boy, was I wrong.

Just because now, you know that you are truly a King's kid, it is not the time to walk in that alone. Now is the time you should get even closer to your Father. Now is the time to pour your heart and soul into the relationship. Now is the time to, not just tell God, but show Him how much you love Him.

Every morning there should be a time of thanksgiving and praises to God. Starting your day with praises automatically raises your power level to handle whatever may lay ahead of you during the day. Take those moments to take your praise time to a higher level.

This is the time you let your heart and spirit burst open with the love you have for your Father. This is the time you move your intimacy level upwards.

Your prayer life should increase because now you are talking to your Father every day. You are seeking His counsel and direction for the day, for every minute of the day.

Your prayers should include the Lord's Prayer (see page 131) daily, but also pray to Him like you would speak to your natural parents.

I was blessed to have a Mother who loved the Lord. She would always sing around the house. Whatever mood she was in, her song of choice would reflect that. I remember going into my parents' bedroom to say good night and sometimes I would find my mother sitting in her chair quietly reading the bible. She would look up, say good night, and go right back to reading. I still have her bible, with all of its marks, today. She even wrote poems that would be on her heart about the pleasure of serving God.

I was also blessed to have a praying Mother. As a very little girl, I can remember my Mother going into her prayer closet (which was our bathroom) and kneeling over the bathtub praying. Sometimes she would make me come in and kneel next to her and she would pray like I wasn't even by her side.

I remember being so glad when she was finished because my prayers lasted 60 seconds… her prayers, not so soon.

But what I really remember is how she prayed for our family and prayed for me. Her voice sometimes got so low I couldn't understand what she was saying (when I was paying attention). Sometimes she would have tears in her eyes when we got up. It was not until years later that I appreciated those times in the bathroom. My Mother had an intimate relationship with God.

Praying with my Mother made me realize several things:

- You can pray and praise God anywhere and anytime.

- Pray with your children, lead by example.

- When you cannot talk to anyone, you can always talk to God. You can always get comfort from the Father.

- It is not a chore but a joy to be able to take time to build an intimate relationship with our Father.

Even though you may have a planned prayer time (talking with God); still, talk to and with Him all the time. At the stop-light, on the job, while cooking dinner, on vacation, break time at work, etc. The bible says, He will hear us. Those prayers could be silent or out loud. He knows our thoughts and our heart.

"This is the confidence we have in approaching God: that if we ask anything according to his will, he hears us." I John 5:14

My Mother knew how to develop and grow her relationship with the Lord. Intimacy will not happen overnight, or because you say I am God's son or daughter. How many parents are disconnected from their children today? Too many.

Intimacy comes after a high level of belief, trust, and faith is established. It is built upon action after action of praises and seeking God, love, and faith. It happens after a time period of consistently seeking His face and working the plan He has given you to fulfill.

And it is not just communicating with your Father on a daily basis, but the quality and spirit in which you pray matters. So many have been trained to pray once a day—morning, noon, or night.

Listen, even diet books will tell you to eat 5 or 6 times a day (small portions) for better health. For better spiritual health and relationship with our Father, simply pray as often as you can.

RELATIONSHIPS

You might be thinking "I have enough friends and relatives in my life. Why do I need to build more relationships?".

Jesus had a mission on this earth. A 3 year mission. In order to fulfill that mission, God instructed Him to choose 12 men to accompany Him on His journey. God knew these men would follow Him and help Him as He helped others.

We, too, must choose wisely who we follow and who we attach ourselves to. The ultimate purpose of our lives is to love one another and spread the love of Christ to all mankind. When we cultivate the right relationships (relationships with our brothers and sisters in Christ), that makes us stronger in our faith and makes our journey much more satisfying and easier.

The type of relationships I want you to think about, are with the persons that love God as much as you do. You want to develop relationships that can empower you to grow spiritually, that can help you fulfill your missions, that will pray with and for you (a prayer partner), have bible studies with you (homegroups), and people that will love you unconditionally because they love you with the love of God.

Having Christian friends who are also on a spiritual journey will give you support, encouragement, and challenge you to reach the goals that the Holy Spirit has placed inside of you.

Here are some ways and places to find those friends who are like-minded and share your love for Christ:

- ✓ Your church
- ✓ Church home-groups
- ✓ Volunteering in a ministry
- ✓ Participate in mission trips

- ✓ Spiritual Mentors
- ✓ Young adult groups
- ✓ Bible study groups
- ✓ Start a group yourself

Having "faith friends", as I like to call them, is just one more way that God helps us walk this journey until Christ's return.

BE HUMBLE

Yes, you are a King or Queen. However, because you come from a royal family, does not mean you are more than or better than others. It means you know who you are, but you don't flaunt a self-important or proud spirit. God wants us to turn to Him in all of our situations. When we are frail, weak, vulnerable, or feeling abandoned, He wants us to come to him for forgiveness, healing, and comfort.

"Humble yourselves, therefore, under God's mighty hand, that he may lift you up in due time." I Peter 5:6

Exercise humility. The Bible says that God gives grace to the humble. What does it really mean to be humble? Dictionary.com says humble means: "not proud or arrogant; modest:". It also says humility is defined as "the quality or condition of being humble; modest opinion or estimate of one's own importance, rank, etc.".

Always confess your needs to God. Let Him know that you truly believe there is nothing impossible if He is in the midst. Your accomplishments are because of Him.

"Talent is God given. Be humble. Fame is man-given. Be grateful. Conceit is self-given. Be careful." John Wooden

You were made for the plan God has just for you. It is time behind to leave doubts, hurts, confusion, self-esteem issues, and anything else that is stopping you from living your best life as you operate in fulfilling your plan. No more excuses. Greatness is your birthright.

Change your mindset and walk in conviction that you were…

GREAT

BEFORE

BIRTH!

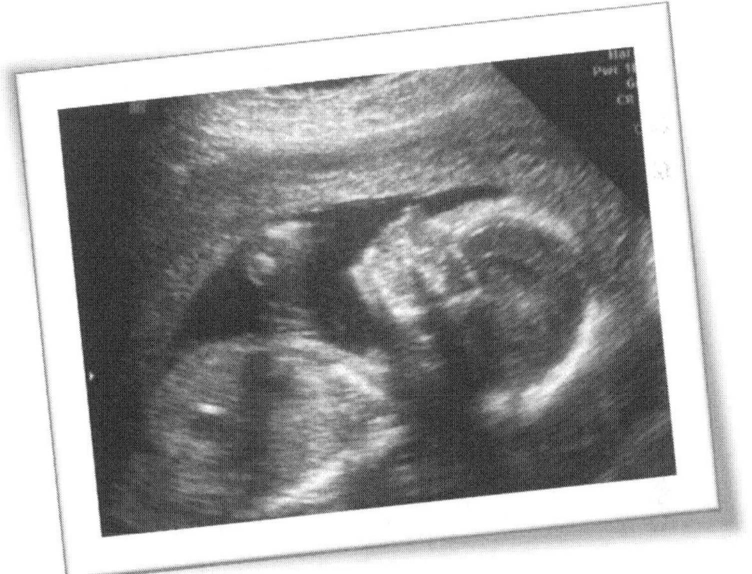

The Lord's Prayer

Matthew 6:8-13

Our Father, who art in heaven,
hallowed be thy Name,
thy kingdom come,
thy will be done,
on earth as it is in heaven.

Give us this day our daily bread.
And forgive us our trespasses,
as we forgive those
who trespass against us.

And lead us not into temptation,
but deliver us from evil.

For thine is the kingdom,
and the power, and the glory,
for ever and ever.
Amen.

What is the Holy Spirit whispering to you, right now, after reading this chapter?

Chapter 7 Notes

Chapter 8
Fifty Affirmations
(Believe)

-dp-

1. I am a child of God
2. I am fearfully and wonderfully made
3. I am confident in my God-given abilities
4. I can do all things through Christ which strengtheneth me
5. I am a lover of my family
6. I am kind
7. I know God holds my future in His hands
8. I am worthy of inevitable success
9. I have skills and talents that can help others
10. I am a beautiful woman
11. I am a handsome man

12. I know that God is able to do exceedingly abundantly above all that I ask or think
13. I will seek God daily
14. I will pray daily for my family
15. I know that my God shall supply all my needs
16. I love myself more and more each day
17. I can turn any obstacle into an opportunity
18. I am an inspiration to others
19. I know that with God, all things are possible
20. I know the joy of the Lord is my strength
21. I know that God has a plan for my life
22. I know that I am loved
23. I know that God performs miracles everyday
24. I will master amazing things through small steps.
25. No negative thought will take root in my mind
26. I will make progress towards my goals
27. I will have a positive impact on someone's life today
28. I claim my Father's power and will remove fear and doubt from achieving my goals today
29. Today, no one will steal my joy
30. I will create such a day that makes me happy to jump out of bed
31. This is the day the Lord has made, and I will rejoice and be glad in it.

32. Everything I need I receive at the right time
33. God and I can handle anything that comes across my path today
34. I am a generous person
35. I am a good listener
36. I am a positive person, and I will attract other positive people today
37. I am strong
38. I am a winner
39. I am comfortable around all types of people and cultures
40. I will be accountable for all of my actions today
41. I am focused
42. I am in charge and determined to meet my goals today
43. I am not a quitter
44. I will not tell God how big my storm is; I will tell the storm how big my God is
45. I will be kind to unkind people
46. I will exceed my own expectations
47. I will make it happen today
48. I will stay faithful and be grateful
49. What I think about, I will bring about
50. I will start today with a new attitude and plenty of gratitude

List Additional Affirmations That Have Blessed You And Helped You To Stay Positive:

Before we part ....

Thank you for reading to the end. Quick question. Who do you know that needs to be a part of our family? Make a list of those you can share the Good News with or even give them a copy of this book.

1. ______________________________

2. ______________________________

3. ______________________________

4. ______________________________

5. ______________________________

6. ______________________________

7. ______________________________

Bibliography

"What Type Of Star Is The Sun?" Science Trends, 15 December 2017, https://sciencetrends.com/kind-star-sun/

"How large is the Sun compared to Earth?" Cool Cosmos https://coolcosmos.ipac.caltech.edu/ask/5-How-large-is-the-sun-compared-to-Earth

"How far away is the Moon?" NASA Science Space Place, 30 September 2019, https://spaceplace.nasa.gov/moon-distance/en/

"It Would Take 200,000 Years at Light Speed to Cross the Milky Way", Space, 2 July 2018, https://www.space.com/41047-milky-way-galaxy-size-bigger-than-thought.html

"Planet Earth Facts", Planet Facts, https://planetfacts.org/planet-earth-facts/

"New Survey Estimates Earth Has 60,065 Tree Species", Smithsonian Magazine, 11 April 2017, https://www.smithsonianmag.com/smart-news/earth-has-60065-tree-species-180962830/

"How Much Water is There on Earth?" USGS Science For a Social Changing World, https://www.usgs.gov/special-topic/water-science-school/science/how-much-water-there-earth?qt-science_center_objects=0#qt-science_center_objects

"World Population" World Population, 16 December 2020, www.worldometers.info

"How Many Babies Are Born Each Day?" The World Counts, 16 December 2020, https://www.theworldcounts.com/stories/How-Many-Babies-Are-Born-Each-Day

"Organismal Biology", Georgia Tech Biological Sciences, 3 January 2019, http://organismalbio.biosci.gatech.edu/biodiversity/animals-invertebrates-2019/

https://www.universetoday.com/

About The Author

Deidre Proctor

Deidre Proctor became a #1 Best Selling Author with the book, “Black Women Speak Out, Stories Of Racial Injustice in America.” She is a Speaker, Philanthropist, Mentor, Coach, and Ministry Leader.

Deidre, a Certified Clarity, Accountability and Business Coach, is the CEO of Deidre Proctor & Associates, LLC.

Deidre realized earlier on that she best fulfills her destiny when she helps others grow.

With over 20 years of experience in sales, marketing, sales training, and strategy development, Deidre’s passion for helping others to achieve their goals has made her a highly sought-after Business Coach and Mentor to women who desire clarity in finding their purpose and those who have goals of starting their own business.

She also created the Personal Passion Signature Program for Female Entrepreneurs. As well as the host of Biblical Principles For Aspiring Entrepreneurs, which is included in her Systematic Success Strategy™.

She is the Co-Founder and CEO of Amazing Retreats International, LLC. Along with her husband, David, she plans and hosts amazing retreats that leave the attendees with ah-ha moments every time. From Women-Only retreats to family retreats to couple retreats to business retreats, she plans each one with her heart and gives attention to the smallest details.

Through their annual signature retreat, The Breathe Retreat, she has brought together Christian women from all walks of life that simply need a break from the hustle and bustle of life. This retreat is only for women who are ready to be refreshed, refocused, and rejuvenated with no distractions from home life or work life.

Deidre is also the Founder and CEO of SHARE YOUR GENIUS. SYG is a group of businesswomen, entrepreneurs, and Ministry Leaders (current, retired, or aspiring), that support each other by sharing the unique skills and talents God has equipped us with. This support includes clarity, mindset, inspiration, empowerment, strategy, and accountability. It's focus – Self-Development, Ministry, and Business.

Deidre is also excited to be a part of the duo team, The Visionary Authors, along with Yolanda "FaithEyes" Bailey.

Her favorite roles are being a Wife, Mother, and Grandmother. She and her husband reside in Texas.

For more information or to contact Deidre:
support@deidreproctor.com
www.deidreproctor.com
www.shareyourgenius.org
www.thebreatheretreat.org

Follow Deidre on Instagram and Facebook:
https://www.instagram.com/coachdeidreproctor/
https://www.facebook.com/clarityandaccountabilitycoach

I have over-the-top love for you and pray God's continual blessings over your life!
Deidre

Made in the USA
Columbia, SC
27 October 2021